REVIV
AND ITS

Revival
by Emyr Roberts

**The Revival of 1762 and
William Williams of Pantycelyn**
by R. Geraint Gruffydd

Evangelical Library of Wales
1981

© Evangelical Library of Wales, 1981
First published—1981

ISBN 0 900898 58 5

All rights reserved. No part of this publication may be reproduced, stored in a retrieval system, or transmitted, in any form or by any means, electronic, mechanical, photo-copying, recording or otherwise, without the prior permission of the Evangelical Library of Wales.

Cover design by
JANET PRICE

Published by the Evangelical Library of Wales,
Bryntirion, Bridgend, Mid Glamorgan, CF31 4DX
Printed by Talbot Printing Co. Ltd.,
Port Talbot, West Glamorgan.

Revival

Emyr Roberts

REVIVAL is probably more remote from the thinking of the churches today than it has been since the beginning of Nonconformity in our land, and certainly since the Methodist Revival of over two centuries ago.* When at the end of October 1904, with the fire of revival in his heart, Evan Roberts felt compelled to leave the preparatory school in Castellnewydd Emlyn, Carmarthenshire, to hold revival meetings in his home town of Casllwchwr in Glamorgan, Evan Phillips the minister, who had celebrated his seventy-fifth birthday the previous week and well remembered the 1859 Revival, recognized the Spirit in the young student and advised him to go. One wonders what advice he would be given today, were he a student under the same spiritual compulsion. Some of the leaders of the 1904 Revival, such as Joseph Jenkins and W. W. Lewis, had been under the tuition of men like Thomas Charles Edwards in Aberystwyth and John Harris Jones in Trefeca, of whom the former had been profoundly affected by the '59 Revival, and the latter a leader in that same Revival. An elder in Caernarfon said in a united prayer meeting in 1904 that he was sure that revival was on the way because he well knew the signs, having experienced the 1859 Revival at the age of twenty-seven. Today, however, there are very few people indeed who are old enough to remember the 1904 Revival. We really need to be reminded of

---

* The 1904 Revival Memorial Lecture of the Presbyterian Church of Wales delivered in English at the Association of the East (at Oswestry) and in Welsh at the Associations of the South (at Cwmdwyfran) and the North (at Prestatyn) during 1978. The lecture was also delivered in English as the Annual Historical Lecture at the Ministers' Conference of the Evangelical Movement of Wales in June 1978.

the dimension of revival; it is a concept which is becoming more and more alien to our whole way of thinking.

Is it necessary here to define the term 'revival'? Anyone who knows what it is to be spiritually awakened, to be made aware of the reality of God and the corruption of his own heart, to taste the forgiveness of sins and the miracle of the new birth, has a key to what happens in revival. Revival is the conviction and conversion of a great number of people, taking place contemporaneously, publicly, and very often dramatically, to the great increase and expansion of the Church. There is no fundamental, qualitative difference between the work of the Spirit in the case of one individual and the work of the Spirit in that which we call revival, but only a difference of degree. Both are the work of the same Spirit of God; both are equally miraculous and supernatural, like the mystery of the wind which 'bloweth where it listeth'. And what people cannot understand they are disposed to criticize and oppose.

It is not surprising, therefore, that revivals have had to be defended against their denigrators: the great Jonathan Edwards, George Whitefield, John Wesley, William Williams of Pantycelyn, Robert Jones of Rhos-lan—men who lived in times of revival and were instruments of revival—had to defend the work against its opponents and detractors. Let us look at some of these criticisms.

The shop is always open

To some, religious revival is an irrelevance because of their view of the Church. Mr. Saunders Lewis has observed, a little mischievously perhaps, that Nonconformity has lived on revivals. This is quite true in a real sense. Our view of revival depends on our view of the Church. The Catholic view is that the Church is essentially an institution—a religious, a divine institution, but an institution not wholly unlike institutions such as the Law or Medicine. Just as these institutions have the resources and provision for your particular needs, so has the Church. She has in her possession, or at her call, everything you need: the time-hallowed forms to worship God, the medicine of the soul in the sacraments, and help in her services to pacify your restlessness, to dispel your anxieties, to uplift your spirit. All the means and resources are there, and at her call. In this sense the Church exists independently of the congregation: if nobody calls, the shop is always open.

As a religious institution the Church also becomes a social and cultural establishment, a bond across the centuries, a reliquary of a people's traditions. Sometimes it becomes the classical expression of a people's identity, as, for instance, the Orthodox Church once was in Russia, or as the Roman Church inclines to be today in Poland and perhaps in Ireland. Let us admit that the Welsh chapel today tends to belong to the same category: it is an essentially Welsh institution, an assertion of our national and cultural identity; indeed, it is so much an integral part of the Welsh way of life that even some of our professing agnostics and atheists still 'belong' to their chapel.

It goes without saying that there is no room for revival in this interpretation of the Church. An institution has no relish for commotion and ferment: it would rather have constancy and stability. To this concept of the Church revival is literally irrelevant, and indeed injurious. When revival has come in the past, and the Church as an institution has found herself unable to tame or control it, she has set her face against it. This is what the Roman Church did to the revival movements in the Middle Ages, and the Anglican Church to the Puritan and Methodist movements.

On the other hand, if we think of the Church as a community of people brought into being by the reviving influences of the Spirit and the Word—in other words, a community of believers—then revival, by definition, is the very principle of her life. The power that brings to life is the power that sustains life. The Church as a body of believers stands in continuous need of the reviving Spirit of God. As a people quickened and made spiritually alive, the very secret of her survival is that the same Spirit of life continues to breathe on her and through her. This has always been so. Even in the Middle Ages, when the Church as an institution was at its strongest, these spiritual breezes breathed upon choice individuals. As they blew here and there in Europe, they brought into being companies of believers such as the Lollards in England, the Waldensians in Italy, the Albigensians in France, and many movements in Central and Eastern Europe. These movements at their beginnings were most often biblical and evangelical, even though some of them later inclined to heterodoxy and error. Since the Protestant Reformation, however, when the Word of God was set free, there has scarcely been a time when the breezes of revival have not been felt to some degree in various parts of the world and, up to the beginning of this century, in Wales most of all. During the period subsequent to the great Methodist Revival of the eighteenth century — between 1785 and the beginning of this century — Gomer M. Roberts has counted no less than sixteen periods of revival in Wales.

A scandal to Christianity?

But apart from this general criticism of revival, which derives from a particular concept of the Church, there are criticisms from other directions. There are those who find in it nothing truly valuable, but regard it as merely a manifestation of crowd hysteria. Peter Price, the most vocal contemporary critic of the 1904 Revival, saw in it nothing but tumult and noise, play-acting and imitation. William Sargant would probably be inclined to see in the excitement of revival times nothing but psychological reflexes to particular stimuli. Then there are many who believe that the definitive criterion of true religion is seemliness and good order, and who abhor any suggestion of extremes of emotion and affections. Such people cannot but be offended by the ferment and untidiness of revival times.

Let us look at some specific examples of 'excesses' during revival periods. What would our reaction be to such 'excesses', I wonder?

At Dinas in Llŷn, when what is called the Llangeitho Revival reached Caernarfonshire, a religious meeting continued for three days and nights. This was probably one of the instances of religious intemperance that prompted Thomas

Morgan, a Glamorganshire man, who had himself been converted under the ministry of Howel Harris and was at that time a nonconformist minister in the West Riding, but had close connections through his wife with Pwllheli, to give as his sober verdict in a letter dated 13 March 1764:

> It appears to all true and serious Christians that they [i.e. the Methodists] are stark mad, and given to a spirit of delusion, to the great disgrace and scandal of Christianity.

George Whitefield, writing to John Cennick, describes how people in Glasgow in June 1742 'by three o'clock this morning were coming to hear the word of God', and how in Cambuslang within a few days William M'Culloch the minister 'preached after I had done till past one in the morning, and then could not persuade the people to depart. In the fields, all night, might be heard the voice of prayer and praise.'

Tomos Elis of Llanystumdwy in Caernarfonshire describes how one Sunday night during the 1859 Revival, as he journeyed home through the villages of Snowdonia, he could hear the sound of prayer and praise along the roads and in the fields from place to place.

Robert Ellis of Ysgoldy in Caernarfonshire relates how a group of men harvesting hay during the Beddgelert Revival of 1817 suddenly threw their rakes in the air, dancing and jumping for joy, after having begun to sing the Welsh hymn:

Mae'r Iesu oll yn hawddgar,	*He's altogether lovely,*
Ydyw'n wir;	*Yes, 'tis true;*
Mae'n well na phethau'r ddaear,	*Than all the world more worthy,*
Ydyw'n wir;	*Yes, 'tis true;*
Enillodd Ef fy nghalon;	*Then fare ye well, dumb idols!*
Ffarwel, eilunod mudion,	*My heart is won by Jesus,*
Mae gwedd ei wyneb tirion,	*His face so fair and gracious,*
Ydyw'n wir,	*Yes, 'tis true,*
Yn foroedd o gysuron,	*An ocean wide of comforts,*
Ydyw'n wir.	*Yes, 'tis true.*

Trans. Edmund T. Owen

E. Morgan Humphreys, the doyen of Welsh journalism in his day, gives an eyewitness account of a revival meeting at

Anfield Road Chapel, Liverpool, in the spring of 1905: the crowds were pressing against the chapel doors, trying to push their way in, and elderly ladies were climbing over the railings to get to the door and, falling on the others, were being thrown inside by the police like sacks of flour.

The poorer language

We could multiply *ad infinitum* such instances of people crowding together and losing their heads in what appears to be sheer religious madness, and we cannot but ask whether there is any difference between this and the frenzies and ecstasies which we associate with the rock and pop groups of our day. On one level there is certainly very little difference. Very probably the immediate sensations, the physical sensibilities and the conscious nervous impressions are very much alike in both. I found light on this in a sermon by C.S. Lewis entitled 'Transposition' [in *Screwtape Proposes a Toast* (Fontana, 1965)]. The tongues phenomenon on the day of Pentecost, he says, might have appeared to an onlooker as nothing but an expression of nervous excitement or hysteria. Then he observes that to express the spiritual through the natural is like translating from a richer to a poorer language. In the poorer language you have to use the same word to express more than one meaning; and it is the same when you try to express the richer world of the spirit through the poorer medium of our physical frame. We have only laughter to express the most ribald revelry and the most godly joy: we have only tears to express the most selfish and worldly grief and the most godly sorrow. Therefore we must not be unduly surprised that spiritual rejoicings are so similar in their manifestations to rejoicings of a very different kind.

Those who criticize revival for what they call its extremes of emotion may well reflect on what we read in the New Testament:

> And the disciples were filled with joy, and with the Holy Ghost.

> In whom . . . ye rejoice with joy unspeakable and full of glory.

> For God, who commanded the light to shine out of darkness, hath shined in our hearts, to give the light of the knowledge of the glory of God in the face of Jesus Christ.
>
> The love of God is shed abroad in our hearts by the Holy Ghost which is given unto us.

It is in words such as these that the apostles of Christ describe the early Christians. And the apostles take it for granted that what they themselves knew of these spiritual experiences, their readers, the ordinary members of the young churches, also knew. People who do not like revivals cannot much like the New Testament.

Dangers and perils

It is quite true that the emotions kindled in revival are not pure, unmixed spiritual experiences. To quote William Williams of Pantycelyn, who is surely our best authority on revival*:

> When our soul came to taste the feasts of Heaven, the flesh also insisted on having its share, and all the passions of nature aroused by grace were rioting tumultuously.

And this at the high tide of the Methodist Revival, of which none can deny that the very powers of the world to come were gloriously at work!

The sublimity of emotions experienced in revivals is illustrated in these words of the Reverend J. T. Job, a minister in Bethesda, Caernarfonshire, at the time of the 1904 Revival:

> One thing I know: *'Thursday night, December the 22nd, 1904'* will be inscribed in letters of fire in my heart for ever! Now, don't ask me to describe *what I felt* that night—*I can never do it!* I can say this: I felt the *Holy Spirit* like a torrent of light causing my whole nature to shake; I saw *Jesus Christ*—and my nature melted at His feet; and I saw *myself*—and I abhorred it! And what more can I say? I can only hope that I am not deceiving myself. But O! the Love of

---

[*See, for example, his *The Experience Meeting — an Introduction to the Welsh Societies of the Evangelical Awakening* (Evangelical Movement of Wales, 1973), translated by Mrs. Bethan Lloyd-Jones — *Ed.*]

God in the Death of the Cross is exceedingly powerful! I have done nothing since Thursday night but sing to myself that hymn, *'O! anfeidrol rym y Cariad!'* &c. ['O! the infinite power of His Love!'] And today I feel *that I belong to everybody.* O! how the Love of Christ *expands* a man's heart!

The critic will claim that this elevated emotional state cannot last. This is generally true. One can hardly live continuously in this fever of exaltation. These experiences are the Delectable Mountains from whose heights we are given a glimpse of Mount Zion: we have to walk generally by faith and not by sight. But on our pilgrimage it is no small thing to catch a glimpse of the beauties of the Heavenly City and to know a foretaste of its felicity and bliss. That we can come down from this height of emotion, and in losing our first joy be tempted to slide back into a worldly spirit, is evident from the many warnings to Christians in the New Testament. We infer that this must have happened even amongst those first Christians. But yet, none can deny that on the pages of the New Testament there is a new quality of life, a new humanity indeed.

It is also true that revival does not abolish at once all the defects of our human nature. The criticism is sometimes made that spiritual awakening is inclined to induce a controversial and opinionated spirit. So it must have been in the New Testament, for we find these early Christians being exhorted against this very thing: 'Foolish and unlearned questions avoid, knowing that they do gender strifes.' Jonathan Edwards observes that the Corinthian Church, left to itself, would have torn itself to pieces, but yet there was a true work of the Spirit there. The apostle greets them as a 'church of God . . . sanctified in Christ Jesus, called to be saints'.

Revival, like conversion, can sometimes induce spiritual pride. In the flush of the great eighteenth-century revival, William Williams warns against this, speaking of a 'raw youth whom no one would entrust to shepherd his sheep, who is today riding high in a boldness of spirit much superior to old ministers who have borne the burden and heat of the day'. Paul warns against appointing a novice in the faith to office in the church, 'lest being lifted up with pride he fall into the condemnation of the devil.' This pride often takes the form of criticizing others for what appears to the new convert to be lukewarmness. In one who has just been swept off his feet in conversion, and has no criterion except his new-found experience against which to evaluate Christian character, this is a failing which can be expected and understood.

These failings, and many others, are the inevitable weaknesses of our sinful human nature. Revival does not perfect saints in a day, any more than conversion does. Jonathan Edwards rightly observes that it is not the work of revival to cultivate moderation and forbearance, but rather to convince and convert, to wake up the drowsy and to quicken the spiritually dead and bring them to God. The cultivation of Christian virtues and the building of sound and sane Christian character is the work, under the blessing of God, of the pastor and teacher.*

The fruits of revival

But, having admitted that there are all these dangers and perils in revival, it still remains true that the very survival of the Church as a body of believers depends utterly on this reviving and life-giving work of the Spirit. Without this reviving work in our hearts, though we have everything else—Christian knowledge and discipline, theological understanding and Bible knowledge—there will be no spiritual life in us. Christian leaders of the past believed implicitly that but for the mercy of God in personal revival and church revival

[*It is interesting to read in this context of the remarks of that witty Calvinistic Methodist minister John Jones (1761-1822) of Edern in Caernarfonshire, probably made at the time of the great 'Beddgelert' Revival which swept North Wales during the last years of his life. Someone had complained to John Jones that it was the young people who were rejoicing and jumping, but that the preachers and elders were not doing so, and therefore were not enjoying the revival. Jones replied thus: 'It is not the old sheep that are to be seen prancing and jumping, but the lambs. Yet the old sheep has its eye ever on the lamb, although she be grazing; and it is very good for that lamb by nightfall that the sheep was grazing to enable her then to give him some milk' (see T. M. Jones, *Cofiant . . . Roger Edwards* (Wrecsam, 1908), p.164—*Ed.*]

there could only be, at best, a dead orthodoxy which would inevitably degenerate into a shallow form of religion utterly lacking in intellectual conviction. One could argue that, generally speaking, the churches in Wales today are drawing perilously close to such a condition. But however serious our declension may be, we may well ponder how much of the Christian Church would remain in our land at all today were it not for the revivals of religion in the past.

Let us consider some of the results of past revivals. There are first of all the great preachers converted during periods of revival. It is said that there were a hundred preachers at the funeral of Daniel Rowland of Llangeitho in October 1790—some of the fruit of the great eighteenth-century revival. Then, from generation to generation, we have such men as Robert Roberts of Clynnog, Christmas Evans, John Elias, John Jones of Tal-y-sarn and David Jones his brother, Thomas John of Cilgerran, John Evans of Eglwys-bach, and Thomas Charles Edwards. These men were all products of revivals: a noble chain of witnesses stretching to the threshold of the revival in the opening years of our present century, of which revival Sidney Evans remarks that it safeguarded the ministry for a whole generation.

Then consider the bare statistics of converts in the revivals. To us in our dispirited condition they sound unbelievable. The 1859 Revival claimed a million converts in America, and a further million in the British Isles, 110,000 of these in Wales alone—a substantial proportion of the one and a quarter million population at the time. During 1882-3, in the revival associated with the name of Richard Owen, there were 1,500 souls added to the churches in South Caernarfonshire, and when the same man came to Denbigh in January 1884, 430 people were added to the churches in the town alone, and many others in the surrounding district. In the last revival, the churches in Rhos, near Wrexham, counted 2,267 converts by the beginning of March 1905. In Anglesey, during the same revival, 2,000 persons were added to the churches, and the number of converts throughout Wales was in the region of 100,000. To our ears these numbers sound staggering, but the truth is that the extraordinary spiritual influences during revivals bring about more results in one week than does a lifetime of labour by dedicated men in ordinary times. And we have to remember the well-known observation that when one person is gained to the Church, it often means the winning of a whole family. How many families who belong to the Church today would be there at all, were it not for the fact that some near or distant ancestor was won to Christianity in a past revival?

Supernatural powers

We must be clear in our minds that revival and what we call an evangelistic crusade are very different things. In revival the supernatural element is uppermost, and the human instruments and activities much less important. The agents of revival are seldom particularly gifted or talented. Dafydd Morgan, so prominent in the 1859 Revival, was a man of great humanity and strong character, but Principal T. C. Edwards, himself deeply influenced in 'Dafydd Morgan's Revival', thus describes the revivalist: 'Before he emerged as a revivalist, Dafydd Morgan was considered an insignificant preacher; and when the tide had ebbed again, the old vessel lay for years on the beach.' Again, Richard Owen was reproached by persons in his own church when he expressed his desire to enter the ministry. What possible qualifications could such a man have, who had only two books in his possession, the Bible and Thomas Charles' catechism? John Williams, Brynsiencyn, says of him that there was scarcely a person of influence in the whole of Anglesey who was warm in his favour, and that many felt it would be a great mistake for this man to enter the pulpit. Then we can think of the last revival, and of all the talent in the Welsh pulpit at the beginning of this century, all its able and learned men; and yet the instrument of the revival was a young collier and blacksmith, who had had only a few weeks in the preparatory school of John Phillips in Castellnewydd Emlyn!

We must also remember that the supernatural spiritual powers rested on leaders of revivals only in one period, or a few periods, of their lives. The Holy Spirit was not at their beck and call. How foolish it is for a man, or a committee of men, to talk and plan as if they could start a revival! One cannot but ask what is coming of the 'Wales for Christ' campaign launched not so very long ago with such a flourish. In revival the one and only essential element is this supernatural element, the Spirit of God coming in power, and of His sheer mercy.

It is striking to observe how small a place there is in revival for human gifts and eloquence. The mighty eloquence of a Whitefield or a Rowland is the exception and not the rule, for very often the greatest influences have accompanied very ordinary powers of speech. One thinks of Jonathan Edwards reading his heavy sermons with a candle in one hand and his script held close to his eyes with the other, whilst his congregation was being overwhelmed by the powers of the Holy Spirit. Or one might consider the beginning of the Beddgelert Revival, which in time spread across the best part of North Wales. It was a Sunday night in August 1817. A company of country folk had gathered from the high valleys and mountain slopes of Snowdonia to the farmhouse of Hafod-y-llan, where a service was being led by a very ordinary lay preacher. To John Hughes, in his three-volume history of Welsh Calvinistic Methodism, *Methodistiaeth Cymru,* the preacher was only 'some brother'; according to Henry Hughes, in his *Hanes Diwygiadau Crefyddol Cymru* ['History of the Religious Revivals of Wales'] he was Richard Williams of Brynengan. The preacher's text was one of Christ's words of invitation to sinners to come to Him. As he warmed to his subject the little congregation felt that it was not Richard Williams at all who was speaking; it was not his voice, not his style, not even his sermon! The preacher himself said afterwards that he was not very sure whether he was preaching or listening to someone else. The service ended in a still silence—no hymn, no singing. There was no appeal. The belief then was that converts were not to 'come forward' in a rush of feeling, but, as it were, in cold blood, in full realization of their commitment. How different this is from our present-day evangelistic crusades! One day the following week, the *seiat* (church meeting) was being held in the chapel, and the two elders, Rhys Williams of Hafod-y-llan, and

William Williams of Hafod-y-rhisgl, sat in the parlour of the chapel-house waiting to go in. One of them peeped through the door to see whether they could begin the service and saw to his astonishment that the place was nearly full. A hymn was given out, but as soon as they stood up to sing the whole congregation broke down in cries and tears. In the words of Robert Ellis of Ysgoldy, quoted by Henry Hughes, 'It transpired that here was a chapel full of people at the end of their tether.' How utterly different is all this from the build-up of personalities, and the accompanying lights and music which we often associate with modern evangelism!

A spirit of prayer

Then again—and I am still emphasizing the supernatural element in revival—there is the spirit of prayer that precedes and accompanies periods of revival. It is so with the revivalists themselves. Dafydd Morgan prayed for ten years for an outpouring of the Holy Spirit. Richard Owen from his very youth was given to much prayer, and would not accept an invitation to hold preaching services in a place unless the people came together to pray before his coming. Evan Roberts prayed for the Holy Spirit for thirteen years, and all the leaders of that same revival—Seth Joshua, Joseph Jenkins, W. W. Lewis, R. B. Jones and others—were men given to much prayer.

Not only is diligence and labour in prayer characteristic of the leaders in a time of revival, but there is also a general spirit of prayer among the people at large. On 1 July 1857, Jeremiah Lanphier, described as 'a quiet and zealous businessman', took up an appointment as city missionary in the North Church of the Dutch Reformed Church in New York. He decided to hold a noonday prayer meeting and distributed a handbill to invite others to join him during the lunch-hour every Wednesday. The first meeting was on 23 September 1857, when just six people came together. The following week twenty persons attended, and the third week about forty people were present. It was then decided to hold the prayer meeting every day. Within six months 10,000 people were gathering in the city every day to pray. Thus began in New York the spiritual awakening which eventually swept throughout America and crossed the seas to the British Isles as the '59 Revival.

At the end of 1904, Henry Williams, the Congregational minister in Colwyn Bay, led twenty prayer meetings in one week. They were held after the revival services, and some of them continued for as long as three hours. On the Wednesday night a hundred people attended, and 250 on the Thursday night, when the meeting continued until after midnight. During that week scores of men and women had voluntarily taken part in prayer.

Christmas Day in 1904 fell on a Sunday. On the Monday, Boxing Day, a prayer meeting was held at 10 o'clock in Salem Chapel, Caernarfon. The Reverend J. E. Hughes relates that a good number had come together, and that the 'unction from the Holy One' was felt to be falling gently and quietly upon the congregation. Another prayer meeting was then announced for the afternoon, and when the time came the spacious building was full: 'a strange sight', he adds, 'on Boxing Day in our town!' The variety entertainment at the Winter Carnival in the famous pavilion, he goes on to say, was 'mortally wounded', and before the end of the week it was discontinued. In the months that followed, two or three prayer meetings were held every day, alternating weekly from chapel to chapel.

On that same Boxing Day, three prayer meetings were held in the village of Rhos, near Wrexham, the evening congregation filling two chapels; and for months after this there were two prayer meetings a day, and three on Saturdays and Mondays. Such a spirit of prayer comes not by the will of man, but is a gift from on high, an offshoot of the divine visitation. Accompanying the spirit of prayer there was also a gift of language and fluency of expression. Sir John Morris-Jones remarked on the fluent and exalted diction in prayer of farm-labourers who had little education but were filled with the spirit of revival.

How do we explain all this—the coming together of thousands of persons in times of revival, with little publicity, no handbills, no posters, no radio or television, and in earlier revivals even with few newspapers? How do we explain the power accompanying some of these leaders, the tremendous and overwhelming sense of the presence of God in the meetings? Whence this spirit of prayer, this will and desire to pray, and the manifest gift of prayer? How do we explain the thousands of genuine conversions, the fact that ungodly and dissolute men were changed overnight to become saints of God and, in time, pillars in His Church? There is only one convincing explanation: a merciful visitation from on high. We have lost to a great degree the dimension of the supernatural from our religion. Revival, by definition, is a supernatural phenomenon. The heart of revival is beyond psychological or sociological explanation.

What of the future?
What are the prospects of revival in our day and age? We should not be light-heartedly optimistic. I say this not because we are too sophisticated and clever; not because we are too modern. No generation is more modern than any other. Modern merely means contemporary. Every generation is modern in its day, and every generation eventually becomes ancient and old-fashioned. But it seems to me that the churches today, by which I mean the main part of the traditional denominations, need more than a revival. We need reformation. We need to discover anew the great central, saving truths of the faith. The Church, always in danger of drifting from these truths which are perpetually a stumbling-block to human wisdom, has had to contend and strive from age to age to defend and maintain them. This was the case even in apostolic times, as we find in the New Testament epistles.

One feels at times today that the battle for the time being is wellnigh lost. We have no theology of revival. That theology, the doctrine of the apostles and the reformers, was under heavy attack in 1904, when what was then known as modernism was rolling in, sweeping and strong. The Reverend William Hobley observed that the 1904 Revival lacked the theological emphasis of the 1859 Revival. He quotes the words of 'a revered elderly minister' that 'it was for the Atonement they gave thanks in '59; but now they give thanks for their own pleasant feelings.' It was surely this theological void, the doctrinal deviation of the times, that accounts for the somewhat disappointing results of that revival even in terms of character building. The converts were often nurtured on doctrines which did not square with their spiritual experience, on a diet consisting of the thin religious hash of a reduced Bible, German philosophy and biblical criticism.

Today our theological condition is even worse. The modernism of the first part of the century has long been discredited. Then we lived through the more biblical theology associated with the names of Barth and Brunner, and this to a large extent gave way eventually to a new radicalism which is even further from the gospel than the old modernism. Today we have almost reached the position where the person who is orthodox in his beliefs and convictions, who stands on the Bible and in the central tradition of the Christian faith, is considered to be a dogmatic reactionary, a stubborn anti-intellectualist, an obscurantist to be pitied and derided. The gospel which brings men to a personal knowledge of Christ and to the joyful experience of the new birth has to be fought for in the very inner councils of the historic denominations. In conditions such as these, his would be a glib and shallow mind that dared to promise smoothly that a revival of vital religion is close at hand.

And yet we have to remember that God is the God of wonders, the God of miracles, the God of gracious and incalculable mercy to the unworthy. Who knows that He may not yet show mercy to a degenerate and apostate people? There never has been, and there never will be, a time when we *deserve* the gracious visitation of His reviving Spirit. The Church will never have anything but its need and poverty to plead before the throne of God, and no other advocate but Jesus Christ the righteous, who is the propitiation for our sins, and not for ours only, but also for the sins of the whole world. We would do well to make it our first priority and concern to plead as a people, 'O Lord, revive thy work in the midst of the years, in the midst of the years make known; in wrath remember mercy.'

The Revival of 1762 and William Williams of Pantycelyn

R. Geraint Gruffydd

AS I thank the committee of the Revival Memorial Fund for their kind invitation to deliver this lecture, I must at the same time admit that I experienced more difficulty than usual in choosing a subject for the lecture.* Revivals have been such an important factor in the recent religious history of Wales that the field is an extremely luxuriant one with a variety of subjects suggesting themselves: the enigma of Evan Roberts's personality, for example, or the background to Richard Owen's thought, or the catalytic influence of 'Dafydd Morgan's Revival' on Welsh nonconformist life. Ultimately, however, I decided to go back to the beginnings of Welsh Methodism and to consider briefly what was perhaps the first distinct, fairly widespread revival in Welsh Methodist history, namely the 'Llangeitho Revival' of 1762-4. I did this because that revival, or rather the reaction to it, inspired William Williams of Pantycelyn—whom we rightly consider our greatest hymn-writer—to write a defence of revival, and the phenomena associated with it, which even today may give us cause to think. I need hardly say how indebted I am in that which follows to the pioneer work on Pantycelyn accomplished by the Rev. Gomer M. Roberts.

* The 1904 Revival Memorial Lecture of the Presbyterian Church of Wales delivered in English at the Association of the East (at Aberystwyth) and in Welsh at the Associations of the South (at Carmarthen) and the North (at Bala) during 1969. The Welsh version of the lecture appeared in *Cylchgrawn Cymdeithas Hanes y Methodistiaid Calfinaidd*, Vols. LIV:3 and LV:1. The lecture was also delivered in English as the Annual Historical Lecture at the Ministers' Conference of the Evangelical Movement of Wales in June 1969. I regret I have been unable to incorporate references to more recent work in the field. My thanks are due to Mr. and Mrs. E. Wyn James for their labours in preparing the text of the lecture for the press.

I mentioned the phenomena associated with the 1762-4 Revival. Some of these phenomena were, of course, well-known from the earliest dawn of the Methodist Awakening in 1735. Time and again Howel Harris records in his journal that, as he preached, 'the Lord came down', and people were visibly affected by his words. Sometimes they would weep and cry out in remorse for their sins and terror at the prospect of the coming Judgement. Sometimes they would shout for joy as they found themselves in possession of the proffered salvation in Jesus Christ — 'my voice was drowned by their cries and Hosannas . . . the Hallelujahs drowned all.' These phenomena, it seems, were especially apparent under the incomparable ministry of Daniel Rowland at Llangeitho and elsewhere. 'At seven of the morning', said George Whitefield in 1743, 'have I seen perhaps ten thousand from different parts, in the midst of sermon, crying "Gogoniant!" "Bendith!" ["Glory!" "Praise!"] — ready to leap for joy.'[1] The evidence of a kinsman of Rowland's in a letter of 1746 is similar, despite the fact that his standpoint is very different from that of Whitefield's:

> While he was performing Divine Service, the people seemed to behave quietly and somewhat devoutly, but as they began to sing, I could hear a voice louder than all the rest crying out 'Rhowch foliant!' ['Give praise!'] and by and by another hollowing 'Rhowch glod!' ['Give honour!']. By this conduct (being yet a mere prelude in comparison of what ensued) I concluded that these two persons might be seized with a fit of the lunacy or frenzy. But as soon as this solemn part of the service was over, Mr. Rowland made a long extempore prayer before his sermon, which prayer, it seemed, worked so upon most part of the audience that some cried out in one corner, 'Rhowch glod!' others in different parts of the church bawled out as loud as possibly they could, 'Bendigedig, rhowch foliant!' ['Glorious, give praise!'] and so on, that there was such a noise and confusion through the whole church that I had much ado, though I stood nigh the minister, to make sense of anything he said. His preaching, again, flung almost the whole society into the greatest agitation and confusion possible: some cried, others laughed, the women pulled one another

> by the caps, embraced each other, capered like, where there was any room, but the perfectionists continued as before their huzzas . . . Surely they are actual instances of perfect enthusiasm. Nay, I never saw greater instances of madness, even in Bedlam itself.[2]

Such manifestations of emotion were, as I have suggested, almost the normal concomitants of preaching and exhorting in the Heroic Age of Welsh Methodism, the fifteen years between 1735 and 1750, before the unhappy schism occurred between Howel Harris and his brethren, and spring turned into sere autumn.

That schism lasted for nine troubled years. Then, in 1759, came the first tentative steps towards reunion, and by 1763 the reunion was complete—or at least as complete as it was ever to be. The Revival of 1762 was both a harbinger of that reunion and a seal upon it. Our primary source of information concerning the revival is *Drych yr Amseroedd* ['The Mirror of the Times'], by Robert Jones of Rhos-lan, which did not appear until 1820 but which (apart from a certain vagueness with regard to dates) is a generally reliable chronicle, largely derived from oral testimony, of the first eighty years of Methodist history. This is what Robert Jones has to say—in translation—of the events of 1762:

> About the year 1762, in the face of great unworthiness and baseness, God remembered His covenant, by visiting graciously a great number of sinners in several parts of Wales; the Sun of Righteousness arose on a great throng of those who sat in the land and shadow of death. In these summer-like days one might say: 'Lo, the winter is past, the rain is over and gone; the flowers appear on the earth; the time of the singing of birds is come, and the voice of the turtle-dove is heard in our land'.
>
> There was a great difference between this revival and that which began at first through [the agency of] Mr. Harris: the mode of proceeding in that was sharp and very thunderous: but in this, as in the house of Cornelius long ago, great crowds magnified God without being able to cease, but sometimes leaping in jubilation as did David before the Ark. Sometimes whole nights were spent with a voice of joy and praise, as a multitude that kept holiday. I heard from a

godly old woman that it lasted three days and three nights without a break in a place called Lôn-fudr in Llŷn, Caernarfonshire, one crowd following the other: when some went home, others came in their place; and although they went to their homes for a while, they could stay there hardly any time before returning. When these powerful outpourings descended on several hundreds, if not thousands, throughout South Wales and Gwynedd, there arose much excitement and controversy concerning the matter; many were struck with amazement and said, 'What can this mean?' 'They are drunkards,' said some. Others said, 'They are mad', very like those [earlier scoffers] on the day of Pentecost long ago: but hardly anyone dared harm them, apart from making them a target for hostile tongues . . .

(It is noteworthy that it was on the day that Mr. W. Williams brought the hymn-book entitled *Y Môr o Wydr* ['The Sea of Glass'] to Llangeitho that the revival broke out, after the long winter which had enveloped the churches because of the schism which has already been mentioned.) [3]

If we are to accept the evidence of Robert Jones, the general course of events was something like this. Some time in 1762 (the book appeared late in 1761), William Williams brought his new collection of hymns, *Caniadau y rhai sydd ar y Môr o Wydr* ['The Songs of those who are on the Sea of Glass'], to Llangeitho. This great hymnal, with its deliberate emphasis on the *mixed* nature of the Christian's inward experience, triggered off an extensive revival which was characterized not only by *gorfoledd* — verbal expression of the joy of salvation—but also by singing and sometimes even by jumping and dancing. (There is some evidence that such singing and dancing had manifested themselves sporadically on previous occasions, but never before on such a scale as this.) [4] This revival was by no means confined to Llangeitho; rather, it spread to several parts of the country, including North Wales—the first time this had happened. Not unnaturally, the singing and dancing associated with the revival attracted a good deal of attention, much of it hostile, but the hostility remained verbal rather than physical. This, in outline, is the picture drawn by Robert Jones of Rhos-lan.

Howel Harris's journal for 1763, the year of the 'Reunion', generally confirms this picture. Several times, as Harris moves again amongst his old friends, he refers to the 'spirit of singing, rejoicing and leaping for joy' which characterized the revival. At first he thought that this excitement had begun through the agency of Daniel Rowland himself, but at the Llansawel Association of 3 August William Williams stated: 'till the Lord did come with these late showers of Revival, all was gone to nothing . . . this was not by any man, but by the Lord Himself, or by some of the meanest of all the exhorters'. One of these 'mean exhorters' may have been William Richard from whom Harris heard later in the year, 29 November, 'of the beginning of this last Revival in Cardiganshire, and how that word went through him when the first cried out at Llangeitho, "I will once more shake the heavens."' (A reference to Hebrews 12:26, 'Yet once more I shake not the earth only, but also heaven.')[5] Whatever Daniel Rowland's exact rôle may have been in this revival (and unfortunately we cannot look to his early biographers for light on this matter because their chronology is so vague),[6] it is almost certain that he lost his curacies at Llangeitho and Nancwnlle as a result: probably during the summer of 1763.

On 13 June of that same summer a letter was sent from Llan-y-crwys, a village in northern Carmarthenshire, to the editor of *Lloyd's Evening Post and British Chronicle,* a London newspaper. The letter, or part of it, appeared in the 27-29 June issue of that paper:

> There is here what some call a great Reformation in Religion among the Methodists, but the case is really this. They have a sort of rustic dance in their public worship, which they call religious dancing, in imitation of David's dancing before the Ark. Some of them strip off their clothes, crying out 'Hosannah!' &c., in imitation of those that attended our Saviour when he rode into Jerusalem. They call this the glory of the latter day; and when any person speaks to them of their extravagance, the answer they give is, 'You have the mark of the enemy in your forehead!' Such is the delusion and uncharitableness of this people!

Exactly two months later John Wesley was in Carmarthen and received an account from a Mr. Evans (of whom nothing is known) of the commotion amongst the Methodists: Wesley's reaction was also negative as may be seen from this entry in his journal (27 August 1763):

> Mr. Evans now gave me an account, from his own knowledge, of what has made a great noise in Wales: 'It is common in the congregations attended by Mr. W[illiam] W[illiams of Pantycelyn] and one or two other clergymen, after the preaching is over, for anyone that has a mind to give out a verse of a hymn. This they sing over and over with all their might, perhaps over thirty, yea forty times. Meanwhile the bodies of two or three, sometimes ten or twelve, are violently agitated; and they leap up and down, in all manner of postures, frequently for hours together.' I think there needs no great penetration to understand this. They are honest, upright men who really feel the love of God in their hearts. But they have little experience, either of the ways of God or the devices of Satan. So he serves himself of their simplicity in order to wear them out, and to bring a discredit on the work of God.

It is only fair to add that when Wesley later met with not dissimilar phenomena among his own followers in Derbyshire, he was somewhat more cautious in his strictures![7]

I should like to summon two further witnesses of the events of 1762-4, both of them Dissenting ministers, and both hostile. The first is David Lloyd, the Arian minister of Llwynrhydowen church in the parish of Llandysul. In a letter to his brother, dated 27 April 1764, he wrote as follows (and here once again the main emphasis is placed on the singing and dancing—or the 'capering', as David Lloyd puts it):

> The Methodists, after having kept quiet for several years, have of late been very active. Their number increases, and their wild pranks are beyond description. The worship of the day being over, they have kept together in the place whole nights, singing, capering, bawling, fainting, thumping and a variety of other exercises. The whole country for many miles round have crowded to see such strange sights [8]

The second Dissenting witness I should like to summon is

Thomas Morgan, a Glamorganshire man who in 1763 became
minister of the nonconformist church at Morley in the West
Riding of Yorkshire. Thomas Morgan's evidence is particularly valuable since it refers to North Wales and confirms
that which Robert Jones of Rhos-lan says about the effect of
the revival in Llŷn—although Thomas Morgan views that
effect in a very different light from Robert Jones. Here is part
of his own summary of a letter which he wrote 13 March
1764:

> By a letter from R[ober]t Hughes to Jane Wilson giving an
> account of the present practices of the Methodists in Llŷn
> (in praise of the work, &c.), it appears to all true and
> serious Christians that they are stark mad, and given up to
> a spirit of delusion, to the great disgrace and scandal of
> Christianity. May the Lord pity the poor Dissenters there! I
> am afraid some of them will fall away, by that strong wind
> of temptation.

And in a letter which he wrote three days later to an aunt,
Thomas Morgan continued to harp on the same subject: 'The
Methodists in Caernarvonshire stark mad, etc.'[9]

The attitude of the two Dissenting ministers, David Lloyd
and Thomas Morgan, to the stirring events of 1762-4 fairly
represents the opinion of the majority of their Dissenting
brethren together with the vast majority of the clergy in the
Established Church — and probably the opinion of the
populace at large also. The practice of jumping in response to
the Word preached, a practice which began in 1762, persisted
well into the last century in many parts of Wales; and the
people who practised it—known as 'Welsh Jumpers' to
distinguish them from their few English counterparts—were
regarded with a mixture of derision and contempt by their
more worldly neighbours. Soon the 'Jumpers' became
something of a tourist attraction, and well-bred young
Englishmen doing the fashionable tour of Wales at the end of
the eighteenth century and the beginning of the nineteenth
would attend meetings of the 'Jumpers' in order to record
their impressions in their journals or even on the pages of the
Gentleman's Magazine.[10] These, as always, had their Welsh
imitators, such as Thomas Jeffery Llewelyn Pritchard, the

author of that interesting novel, *The Adventures and Vagaries of Twm Shôn Catti* (Aberystwyth, 1626), who once referred in a poem [11] to

> [The] jumping fanatics, whose dolorous yell
> Remind of the fabled vile orgies of hell!

The 'Jumpers' even found their way inside the covers of ecclesiastical reference books, such as those of Charles Buck and John Evans, Islington, where it is suggested that jumping formed an essential part of their worship. And indeed, if one looks today in *The Oxford Dictionary of the Christian Church* one finds under the catchword 'Jumpers' the following entry:

> A nickname of the Welsh Calvinistic Methodists, from their former custom of 'leaping for joy' at their meetings.

It is probably true that the majority of 'Jumpers' were Calvinistic Methodists, but not all: the practice spread to the other denominations as they too became imbued with the spirit of Methodism. A fascinating late glimpse of the practice is afforded by John Lewis (*Ap Cledan*) in a narrative of the Llanilar Association of 1851. In that Association Lewis Edwards had preached with exceptional fervour on the majesty of God and the congregation's emotions had been deeply stirred; after him William Roberts of Amlwch preached, briefly, and gave out *'Newyddion braf a ddaeth i'n bro'* ['Good news has come to our land'] as the closing hymn:

> As they sang *'Caiff carcharorion fynd yn rhydd'* ['Prisoners shall be set free'], they were indeed set free. Yes, set radically free. Such excitement, such jumping and exulting I never saw either before or since! Old men and old women clasping each other's hands and leaping like roe deer. Many of these were from the neighbourhood of Mynydd Llyn Eiddwen and Llangeitho. I knew them by their dress. Many of them wore clogs. They jumped wonderfully in their clogs. I can offer no explanation for this except that the new nature in them must have been drawing them upwards in a most powerful manner. I have seen praise before this and after this, but jumping and leaping this time only. Oh! what a relief it was for thousands to give vent to the spiritual energy which was in their breasts. Some weeping,

some singing, others exulting and very many doing this while 'leaping and praising God'. This was a meeting to be remembered for ever![12]

And all this—the singing as well as the jumping—began with the Llangeitho Revival of 1762-4.

It is to the everlasting credit of the Methodist Fathers, including Thomas Charles, that they refused to condemn these extraordinary expressions of emotion which first became part of the Welsh Methodist scene in 1762. These Fathers were mostly clergymen who had received a classical education of sorts and it is probable that their instinctive reaction to all these expressions of emotion would have been to designate them as excess and fanaticism and to do their best to stamp them out forthwith. They never, to my knowledge, attempted to evoke these expressions of emotion deliberately, but neither did they condemn them. Indeed, when pressed, they were willing to defend them. And it is with the earliest of these defences, that of William Williams of Pantycelyn, that I want to remain for a while.

This defence was written in the form of two pamphlets.[13] The first appeared in 1762, entitled

Llythyr Martha Philopur at y Parchedig Philo Evangelius ei Hathro. Yn mynegi iddo ei phrofiad, a'r testunau hynny o'r Ysgrythur a ddaeth i'w chof, i gadarnhau y gwaith rhyfeddol ac anghynefin o eiddo'r Arglwydd, a ymddangosodd ar eneidiau lluoedd o bobl yn Sir Aberteifi, ac sydd yr awron yn tannu ar lled i eglwysi cymdogaethol.

which might be translated 'The letter of Martha Philopur to the Reverend Philo Evangelius her Teacher. Relating to him her experience and those texts of Scripture which came to her memory, to confirm that wonderful and strange work of the Lord's which appeared upon the souls of multitudes of people in Cardiganshire, and which is now spreading abroad into neighbouring churches'. The second pamphlet, which appeared in the following year, is simply entitled *Ateb Philo-Evangelius i Martha Philopur* ['The Reply of Philo-Evangelius to Martha Philopur']. These pamphlets are the first original prose writings of Williams to appear. When he wrote them he was between 45 and 46 years of age and at the height of his powers. They reveal that he was indisputably a prose-writer of the first order although, characteristically, careless of detail. But it is with the contents of the pamphlets rather than their style that we are concerned for the present. In the first pamphlet, Martha Philopur, who represents the Methodist convert, tells Philo-Evangelius, who represents the Methodist exhorter or clergyman, how her conversion came about. She describes the agonies she suffered under conviction of sin and the overwhelming joy of knowing that her sins were forgiven. In the glow of this joy she had often praised God publicly and even leapt in exultation. (There follows an exceptionally fine passage describing how her whole personality was exalted in the surge of this experience.) Now, as a result of the revival, this same joy had been shared by thousands of others. 'A new work is in progress; since it began hosts are being convicted.' But some opposed this work and this causes Martha to search the Scriptures in order to test the validity both of her own experience and actions and of those of her friends. She cites sixteen texts or groups of texts from the Old Testament and the New, which confirm her in her belief that it is proper for those who have tasted salvation to express their gratitude by crying out, by singing their praise to God, by clapping their hands and even by jumping for joy. Had not King David, for example, danced before the Ark and rebuked Michal, Saul's daughter, for mocking him for doing so (2 Sam. 6:20-3)? Finally Martha asks Philo-Evangelius whether he approves of her exegesis.

In his reply Philo-Evangelius criticises Martha's letter on account of its brevity but excuses her on the grounds that she is, after all, only a woman! He does not intend defending any error, but (in his opinion) God never works in the world without Satan interfering. *Mae cymysg yn y cyfan is yr haul* ['There is a commixture in all things under the sun']—an epigram worthy of Morgan Llwyd, that great Puritan prose-writer, himself. This commixture comes about not only because of Satan's wiles but also because the excitement of the revival affects hypocrites as well as saints ('the sound of the wind comes to the ears of the hypocrites also, and works somewhat upon their natural passions; and then they are like a ship before the wind, without any ballast but under full sail, in danger of being broken upon the rocks or driven into havens to which they do not belong'); another reason for the commixture is that the natural passions may supplant the spiritual even in the saints. But this commixture does not mean that God is not genuinely at work, as He had been in the recent revival even though the mode of that revival was entirely new. There follows a fine description, which I wish I had time to quote at length, of the spiritual deadness of the land before the revival and its spiritual vitality afterwards —and that in both North and South Wales. *O hafddydd! fe ddaeth, fe ddaeth!* ['O summer's day! it has come, it has come!'] Why should anyone oppose the revival solely on account of the exceptional manifestations of emotion associated with it, especially those who previously had prayed fervently for its coming? Then Philo-Evangelius tries to justify those manifestations rationally: it is natural for lovers to praise their loved ones; it is fitting that our bodies, including our tongues, should be at God's service; it is fitting that we should be bold in that service; and it is natural, since emotions affect bodily actions, that 'people who are full of the love of God should sing, praise, leap for joy, laugh aloud and sound out praise to God'. From the appeal to reason Philo-Evangelius turns to the evidence of the Scriptures and alludes to the outward means used to arouse religious emotion under the Old Dispensation, in contrast with the inward action of the Holy Spirit after Pentecost. Then follows a brief outline of church history (the orthodox Protestant version as established by the Centuriators of Magdeburg in the sixteenth century) in which the Welsh Awakening of 1735/8 is placed in its world context and the sad effects of the schism of 1750 stressed. Then came the Revival of 1762: 'God was its sole author; and it is the same as that which has been from the days of the Apostles until now'. Although Philo-Evangelius concedes that some of the singing and jumping associated with the revival may have been produced by 'the heat of natural passions rather than the fulness of the Spirit of God', yet he dismisses brusquely those professors of religion who were prepared to condemn the revival unconditionally on account of the singing and leaping. Their trouble, he says, is this: 'their religion is in their understanding only, and has never ascended into their hearts ... With the heart man believes unto righteousness; that men have believed some form of doctrine, however true that may be, if the principles which he has received with his understanding have not become rooted in his heart, so that he loves the Son of God, rejoices in His salvation, denies himself, takes up his cross, follows the Lamb through all his tribulations, then his knowledge only serves to puff him up'. Such people feel more at home in the company of worldlings than in that of true believes. And here we have one of the little cameos in which Williams delights. Pneumaticus (a man full of the Spirit) preaches, and the effects associated with the revival follow: singing, leaping and even prostration. 'The place all that time was full of the presence of God'. But there is in the congregation a gentleman named Formalistus and his wife Florida (occasional auditors at the Methodist meetings), and they are highly offended. Away they go to take tea with the Vicar, to gossip about their neighbours and, of course, eloquently to condemn the 'hypocrites' in the meeting house. Then, after tea, they accompany the Vicar to church, to Evening Prayer, where they respond with unction to the Vicar's exhortation (from the Book of Common Prayer) that the people should praise God, and rejoice in Him and even clap hands and sing His praises with shouts of joy — exactly those things which the 'hypocrites' in the meeting house had been practising. 'O Martha! Martha!' says Philo-Evangelius, 'there is a hundred times more of hate towards the Son of God than there is of love towards Him'. Finally Philo-Evangelius stresses that it is not by outward signs alone that he judges the revival to be essentially a work of God. In the first instance, the people affected by it are thoroughly reformed in their way of life. Secondly, they are fervent for, not the secondary or erroneous doctrines, but 'for the primary doctrines regarding salvation', and particularly the doctrine of free grace. Thirdly, they are impeccably orthodox in their view of Christ's person. And lastly, they and they alone were suffering persecution at that time—even the Quakers were left in peace! This leads Philo-Evangelius to warn Martha to expect 'a bitter winter after such a comfortable summer as this' and that the love of many would grow cold. 'Despite all this God will stand by His people . . . Those who fall shall He raise to better things, those who stand shall fear: both will sing together'. In a kind of postscript, directed specifically at the Dissenters, Williams translates— rather badly—a short passage justifying what may be called 'holy disorder' at a time of revival from the pamphlet by Jonathan Edwards, the revivalist and great theologian from New England, *The Distinguishing Marks of a Work of the Spirit of God*, which first appeared in 1741.

That is a rather bare summary of Williams's defence of the phenomena associated with the Revival of 1762-4. On many counts it is a remarkable piece of work, although brief. Its debt to Jonathan Edwards is certainly greater than is implied by the postscript alone. Of the works written by Edwards on revival, Williams was familiar not only with the *Distinguishing Marks* but also with *A Faithful Narrative of the Surprising Work of God in the Conversion of Many Hundred Souls in Northampton and the Neighbouring Towns and Villages* (1736) and with *Some Thoughts concerning the Present Revival of Religion in New-England* (1742). To my knowledge, Williams was not familiar with Edwards's masterpiece on this subject, *A Treatise concerning Religious Affections* (1746).[14] Jonathan Edwards was not only the greatest thinker of the Methodist Awakening in any country, he was also the first theologian seriously to consider the theology of revival as a phenomenon of church life.[15] It says much for Williams's theological acumen that he perceived Edwards's importance in this respect—although it is only fair to remember that close relationships obtained, through both visits and correspondence, between the Revivalists of the Old World and those of the New (Scotland and the Erskine brothers would probably have been the link in this case). From Edwards, as well as from his own experience, Williams learned of the importance of revival as an instrument of God's purpose for His church. From Edwards he learned also that revival is always a mixed or disfigured work of God—but

God's work nevertheless. He may have gone further than Edwards in his justification of the manifestations of emotion associated with revival, possibly because these manifestations were more prominent in Wales than in New England—although it is interesting to remember that Edwards's wife Barbara, to whose experience (without naming her) he devotes a whole section in *Some Thoughts concerning the Present Revival*, sometimes felt constrained to jump for joy when meditating on God's grace:

> Animal nature was often in a great emotion or agitation, and the soul so overcome with admiration, and a kind of omnipotent joy, as to cause the person, unavoidably, to leap with all the might, with joy and mighty exultation.[16]

The *Llythyr* and *Ateb* were not the only apologies which Williams wrote for the phenomena associated with revival. In 1764, in an elegy for the Rev. Lewis Lewis of Llanddeiniol—one of the remarkable collection of elegies he wrote in celebration of his fellow-workers in the Awakening, the *bardd teulu* ('household poet') of the new Heroic Age—Williams made a point of asking the dead man whether singing and dancing were acceptable in heaven, and received a strongly affirmative answer.[17] Twenty years later, at a time of renewed religious excitement, an anonymous 'gentleman' (possibly another William Williams, a Dissenting minister and Justice of the Peace from Pembrokeshire but living in Cardigan) wrote a poem deploring the antics of the enthusiasts, and Williams replied with a long poem—some 276 lines—in which he strongly rebukes the 'gentleman' for his ignorance of the scriptural precedents for the behaviour which he condemned.[18] At about the same time, possibly to the same 'gentleman', Williams wrote a shorter poem on the same theme, which concludes with the following unecumenical stanzas:

> Paham danodi ddawnsio
>   O flaen y delyn fawr?
> Fel 'r oedd yr hen broffwydi,
>   'R un Ysbryd sydd yn awr!
> Plant trythyll Eglwys Loegr,
>   'R un ysbryd â thydi,
> Sy'n torri'r hais a jigo
>   Rownd pedwar a rownd tri.
>
> Am hynny taw, ddyn ynfyd,
>   Cymer y Beibl mawr
> A darllen ef yn fanwl
>   A'th ddeulin ar y llawr.
> Cei weled, [d]i, fod crefydd,
>   Pan fo hi o'th fewn yn dân
> Yn peri [i]'r corff gydseinio,
>   Fel ag 'bu rhai o'th fla'n.[19]

Why dost object to dancing
 The stringèd harp before?
The selfsame Spirit moves us
 As with the seers of yore!
It is the Church of England,
 Her wayward sons like thee,
Who strain their ribs with jigging
 A fourstep round and three.

So, foolish man, stop railing
 And take the sacred Book
And read with care its pages,
 Go pray within thy nook.
Thou'lt see that true religion
 When once it warms thy soul
Soon has thy frame responding,
 As with the saints of old.

Trans. Edmund T. Owen

Finally, John Owen of Thrussington records an anecdote or illustration of Williams's which touches upon the same theme, but with the emphasis this time on the danger of self-deceit amongst people whose emotions had been deeply touched—although it is not suggested for a moment that deep emotions in themselves are a sign of hypocrisy:

> It is said that on one occasion, a respectable person remonstrated with Williams on the subject [namely the practice of leaping], and endeavoured to persuade him to discountenance the practice, alleging that it was very unbecoming, and that many who had engaged in it had been known to have afterwards fallen away and become wholly irreligious. After having listened attentively to what this gentleman had to say, Williams spoke to him somewhat in this manner:
>
> 'There were three people, two men and a woman, living on the side of the same hill, who began the world nearly at the same time. Their names were Evan, Thomas and Betty. When they went there to live, each of them borrowed a hundred pounds. They thought that they could in time by thrift and industry be able to repay this money: but instead of being successful, the three were very unfortunate. And in course of time they were threatened with law: and at last the bailiffs came upon Evan to put him in prison. And as he was going with them, they passed by the house of Sir John Goodman, who lived on the other side of the hill: and they met Sir John himself. "Well," said he, "where are you going, Evan?" Evan respectfully replied and said, "Oh, Sir John, I am obliged to go to prison for debt. It is just, it is right, I confess; for I owe the money: but I have no hope of repaying it." "Indeed, indeed," said Sir John, "I am very sorry for you: but how much is your debt?" "A hundred pounds," said Evan, "and the costs." Then Sir John said, "I will pay thy debt, Evan, and the costs too"; and turning

to the bailiffs, he said, "Let him go, I will be answerable for him." Evan of course felt more than he could well express; and having thanked Sir John in the best manner he could, he returned home. Having reached the top of the hill above his house, he stopped and cried out with all his might, "Thanks, thanks to Sir John Goodman!" Betty heard him and wondered greatly. She however went up to him, and enquired the reason: and when he told her what Sir John had done for him, she also joined him and shouted, "Thanks to Sir John Goodman!" Soon after they were observed by Thomas. He also went up to know the cause: and when it was told him, he could not do otherwise than exclaim with them, "Thanks, thanks, thanks, to Sir John Goodman!" But in course of a short time the demand for the money was made on Thomas and Betty, and as they had nothing to pay, they were apprehended and put in prison, and there they both died. Though they joined Evan in rejoicing, they never applied to Sir John Goodman.' [20]

Parallel with his defence of the phenomena associated with revival, Williams also mounted an attack on the opposing standpoint of John Glass and Robert Sandeman, two Scots who were a thorn in the side of the Methodist movement during the sixties, particularly during the period 1763-6. Sandeman taught that faith—the faith which justifies—is nothing more than a bare intellectual assent to the truths of the Gospel, involving neither the will nor the emotions.[21] This concept was entirely repugnant to Williams and he fought against it with all his might—and he was no mean fighter! In an elegy he wrote in 1766 he declares himself (with his tongue very much in his cheek, I should say) tired of the fray and desirous only of a quiet, happy place to which he may retreat:

Nefol nyth, hyfryd byth, tawel a dirgel,	*Heavenly nest, sweet, hidden, peaceful,*
Maes o stŵr y byd a'r rhyfel,	*Far from madding crowd and battle,*
Terfysg Sandeman a'r cythrel! [22]	*Noise of Sandeman and devil!*
	Trans. Edmund T. Owen

Although Williams was undoubtedly the chief defender of the Welsh 'Jumpers' from 1762 onwards, he was not the only one. Even an occasional Independent like Dafydd Jones of

Caeo, and an occasional Baptist like Christmas Evans, were prepared to join the ranks of the defenders.[23] More important from our point of view is the fact that both Daniel Rowland and Howel Harris substantially agreed with Williams. Nathaniel Rowland once told John Owen of some correspondence which his father had had with John Thornton, a rich Englishman and a member of William Romaine's congregation in London (it was he who offered Rowland the Rectory of Newport, Pembs., in 1769). Thornton did not like the jumping and had repeatedly urged Rowland to condemn the practice. At length Rowland answered:

> You English blame us, the Welsh, and speak against us and say 'Jumpers! Jumpers!' But we, the Welsh, have something also to allege against you, and we most justly say of you, 'Sleepers! Sleepers!'[24]

This silenced Mr. John Thornton! Finally Howel Harris, preaching at Llansawel on 16 February 1763 spoke as follows:

> This work of singing, if God comes in this way for a time for some wise purpose, who will hinder Him? His saving and usual way is to come without any outward appearance, calmly, quietly and still. If a man was in Carmarthen jail for debt, and never hoped to come from there, and beyond expectation a relative from the East Indies, hearing of his circumstances, would come and pay his debt and release him, would you blame him much if he could not contain himself for some time, but did leap as David before the Ark? Would you not excuse him? The case here is beyond this![25]

It is doubtful, however, whether Harris was ever as whole-hearted in his endorsement of the 'Jumpers' as Williams. Some years later (13 February 1770) he was to confess, 'I do not understand these outward frames of jumping.'[26] The tradition of Harris's Family at Trefeca was on the whole opposed to too blatant a manifestation of emotion, which is presumably why Williams called the Family *defaid . . . oerion, hesbion, sych* ['cold, barren, dry . . . sheep'] in his elegy for Harris.[27]

Has the Revival of 1762 and the controversy which followed it any relevance for us today? I believe that it certainly raises some pertinent questions. In the first instance it causes us to ask ourselves whether we believe with William Williams and Jonathan Edwards that revivals have a central place in God's purpose for His church; in the words of Edwards that 'the work of redemption in its effect has mainly been carried on by remarkable communications of the Spirit of God'[28], that is, by revivals. Thomas Charles, the architect of the Calvinistic Methodist Connexion, certainly believed this fervently: he wrote these words in 1792:

> I am persuaded that, unless we are favoured with frequent revivals, and a strong powerful work of the Spirit of God, we shall in a great degree degenerate and have only a 'name to live': religion will soon lose its vigour; the ministry will hardly retain its lustre and glory; and iniquity will of consequence abound.[29]

Do we agree with him, or are we among those who trust in chariots and horses rather than in the name—and power—of the Lord our God? We may agree with him without having to believe that any future revival will be exactly like any revival of the past, or that revival will necessarily solve all our problems—indeed, it would certainly bring fresh problems in its wake, since all revivals, as Jonathan Edwards continually stresses, are *mixed* works of God's Spirit.

Secondly, the Revival of 1762 raises in an accute form the whole question of the rôle of the emotions in religious life. Whereas Edwards and Williams would deny absolutely that strong emotions are in themselves evidence of genuine faith—and indeed supply tests for assessing such emotions— yet both would expect true faith to give rise to strong emotions. 'True religion, in great part, consists in the affections,' said Jonathan Edwards in his *Treatise*.[30] And as we have seen, Williams went so far as to justify manifestations of emotion which may appear to us, in our Laodicean state, to be quite ludicrous. Why are strong emotions so rare among us? Is it simply because, as Dr. Geoffrey Nuttall seems to suggest in his brilliant little book on Howel Harris, that we no longer '*believe* that we are lost without Christ or delivered by Him'?[31] Or is it because we are in the grip of a kind of practical Sandemanianism, a crass over-intellectualism which stifles emotion at source and grieves the Spirit? This may indeed be a greater hindrance to the work of God among us than our present state of theological anarchy and our tragic abandonment of the great tradition of moderate Calvinism in which we were nurtured as a Connexion. I think, were I to hear one day that one of our congregations had started to weep spontaneously in a meeting, that I might start jumping for joy myself!

If we come to believe that revival may, after all, be the only effective answer to our problem, the only practical thing we can do is to pray. Revivals are at God's disposal; they are not man-made. Edwards in particular lays great stress on *persistent* prayer for revival.

> It is very apparent from the word of God, that He is wont often to try the faith and patience of His people, when crying to Him for some great and important mercy, by withholding the mercy sought for a season; and not only so, but at first to cause an increase of dark appearances. And yet He, without fail, at last succeeds those who continue instant in prayer, with all perseverance, and 'will not let Him go except He blesses'.[32]

If we learn to pray like this, perhaps we too, in our time, may yet be able to say as William Williams of Pantycelyn was able to say in 1763: *O hafddydd! fe ddaeth, fe ddaeth!* ['O summer's day! it has come, it has come!'].

Notes

1. John Gillies, *Memoirs of the Life of . . . George Whitefield* (London, 1772), p.131n.; quoted by Geoffrey F. Nuttall, *Howel Harris, 1714-1773: The Last Enthusiast* (Cardiff, 1965), p.56. The language and punctuation of all quotations have been standardized.

2. J. H. Davies, 'Daniel Rowland: Contemporary Descriptions (1746 and 1835)', *Cylchgrawn Cymdeithas Hanes y Methodistiaid Calfinaidd*, i (1916), p.54.

3. *Drych yr Amseroedd Robert Jones, Rhos-lan*, ed. G. M. Ashton (Cardiff, 1958), pp.84-6; with the last paragraph, compare *Trysorfa*, ii (1809-13), p.450. For a discussion on Robert Jones as a historian, see J. E. Caerwyn Williams, 'Robert Jones, Rhos-lan: yr Hanesydd', *Transactions of the Caernarvonshire Historical Society*, xxiv (1963), pp.153-95.

4. See note 2 above, and also *Howell Harris, Reformer and Soldier (1714-1773)*, ed. Tom Beynon (Caernarfon, 1958), p.157.

5. *ibid.,* pp.187-9, 209.

6. John Owen of Thrussington, in his *A Memoir of the Rev. Daniel Rowlands* (London, 1840), makes mention of a number of revival episodes in Rowland's life which could easily be connected with the commotion of 1762-4; but one cannot be sure.

7. *The Journal of the Rev. John Wesley*, ed. N. Curnock (London, 1909-16), v, pp.27-8; vii, pp.152-3.

8. *Lloyd Letters (1754-1796)*, ed. G. Eyre Evans (Aberystwyth, 1908), p.52.

9. NLW, MS. 5453C; quoted in R. T. Jenkins, *Yng Nghysgod Trefeca* (Caernarfon, 1968), p.48. It may be worth adding that the names of some of those involved in the revival in Caernarfonshire at this time were preserved by oral tradition and recorded during the last century: William Owen of Bodlas near Garn Fadrun, who during the time of the excitement at Lôn-fudr—alluded to by Robert Jones—spent the whole of the three days and three nights in chapel, returning home only for meals; Catherine Prichard of Clynnog, who was the first to commence jumping in Caernarfonshire, so that the word went around that a woman from Clynnog had lost her senses while listening to the Methodist preaching; and also the two evangelical clergymen, Richard Nanney of Clynnog, whose faith revived as his years declined—he died 1767—and Evan Hughes, 'Hughes Fawr', curate of Llaniestyn, Llandegwning and Penllech in Llŷn between 1762 and 1764. See Henry Hughes, *Hanes Diwygiadau Crefyddol Cymru* (Caernarfon, [1906]), pp. 149-50, 153-4.

10. D. E. Jenkins, *The Life of the Rev. Thomas Charles* (Denbigh, 1908), ii, pp.360-84.

11. *Cylchgrawn Cymdeithas Hanes y Methodistiaid Calfinaidd,* ii (1916-17), p.64.

12. *ibid.*, xxiv (1939), pp.38-9.

13. A convenient reprint of both is available in *Gweithiau William Williams Pantycelyn,* vol. ii, ed. Garfield H. Hughes (Cardiff, 1967), and has been used here.

14. *ibid.*, p.31 (it is the *Faithful Narrative* which is praised by 'Dr. Watts, and Dr. Guise'); Gomer M. Roberts, *Y Pêr Ganiedydd,* i (Aberystwyth, 1949), p.85. I am grateful to the Rev. D. Elwyn Edwards, our chief authority on the influence of Edwards in Wales, for confirming that he also knows of no reference to the *Treatise* by Williams.

15. J. I. Packer, 'Jonathan Edwards and the Theology of Revival', *Increasing in the Knowledge of God: Papers read at the Puritan and Reformed Studies Conference, 20th and 21st December, 1960* (London, 1961), pp.13-28.

16. *The Works of Jonathan Edwards,* ed. E. Hickman (Edinburgh: Banner of Truth Trust, 1974), i, p.376.

17. *Gweithiau Williams Pant-y-celyn,* ed. N. Cynhafal Jones (Holywell and Newport, 1887-91), i, pp.448-59.

18. *ibid.*, pp.619-26.

19. Quoted (and modernized) from Cambridge University Library Add. MS. 6172 in order to compare that version with the one from NLW Add. MS. 269A, quoted by Gomer M. Roberts, *Y Pêr Ganiedydd,* ii (Aberystwyth, 1958), pp.164-5.

20. *op. cit.,* pp.206-7.

21. D. Martyn Lloyd-Jones, 'Sandemanianism', *Profitable for Doctrine and Reproof* [Puritan Conference Report, 1967] (London, 1968), pp.54-71.

22. Gomer M. Roberts, *op. cit.,* i, p.145 (the verse is omitted in Cynhafal Jones's edition!).

23. Gomer M. Roberts, *Dafydd Jones o Gaeo* (Aberystwyth, 1948), pp.30-31; Henry Hughes, *op.cit.,* pp.240-8.

24. John Owen, *op. cit.*, pp.85-6. [It is interesting to note in this context the opposition of another prominent English evangelical, the Rev. Rowland Hill (1744-1833), to the practice of jumping. In *The Journal of the Rev. John Wesley* (vol. v, p.27), the following foot-note is to be found: '"Let us have no more of this mummery and nonsense," said Rowland Hill when the Jumpers commenced their antics in one of his services in Wales.'—*Ed.*]

25. Tom Beynon, *op. cit.*, p.157.

26. *Cylchgrawn Cymdeithas Hanes y Methodistiaid Calfinaidd*, xxix (1944), p.47.

27. cf. Gomer M. Roberts, *Bywyd a Gwaith Peter Williams* (Cardiff, 1943), pp.49-50.

28. *The Works of Jonathan Edwards*, i, p.539; see J. I. Packer, *op. cit.*, pp.24-25.

29. D. E. Jenkins, *op. cit.*, ii, p.98.

30. *The Works of Jonathan Edwards*, i, p.237.

31. *op. cit.*, p.47.

32. *The Works of Jonathan Edwards*, ii, p.312; see J. I. Packer, *op. cit.*, pp.27-8.